Cricut Project Ideas

D1382694

A detailed guide to start creating
quickly amazing projects for yourfamily
and friends. Includes 500 DIY ideas
for Cricut Maker, Explore Air 2 and
Design space.

By: Lara Craft

Copyright 2020 by Lara Craft
All rights reserved

This content is provided with the sole purpose of providing relevant information on a specific topic for which every reasonable effort has been made to ensure that it is both accurate and reasonable. Nevertheless, by purchasing this content you consent to the fact that the author, as well as the publisher, are in no way experts on the topics contained herein, regardless of any claims as such that may be made within. As such, any suggestions or recommendations that are made within are done so purely for entertainment value. It is recommended that you always consult a professional prior to undertaking any of the advice or techniques discussed within.

This is a legally binding declaration that is considered both valid and fair by both the Committee of Publishers Association and the American Bar Association and should be considered as legally binding within the United States.
The reproduction, transmission, and duplication of any of the content found herein, including any specific or extended information will be done as an illegal act regardless of the end form the information ultimately takes. This includes copied versions of the work both physical, digital and audio unless express consent of the Publisher is provided beforehand. Any additional rights reserved.

Furthermore, the information that can be found within the pages described forthwith shall be considered both accurate and truthful when it comes to the recounting of facts. As such, any use, correct or incorrect, of the provided information will render the Publisher free of responsibility as to the actions taken outside of their direct purview. Regardless, there are zero scenarios where the original author or the Publisher can be deemed liable in any fashion for any damages or hardships that may result from any of the information discussed here. Additionally, the information in the following pages is intended only for informational purposes and should thus be thought of as universal. As befitting its nature, it is presented without assurance regarding its prolonged validity or interim quality. Trademarks that are mentioned are done without written consent and can in no way be considered an endorsement from the trademark holder.

Table Of Contents

INTRODUCTION

Perhaps you've just purchased your first Cricut® or you've had one for some time but haven't tried it out yet, or you are fairly skilled but aren't sure how to use the Design Space.

This book will teach you everything you need to know about using Cricut Design Space™ like a pro.

Cricut has come a long way since it was first introduced in 2006 by Provo Craft & Novelty, Inc, and has undergone many changes. The company has released many versions of its die-cutting machine as its popularity among crafters has soared. From its inception, the Cricut has provided many ways for a crafter to make beautiful things and sell them for a nice profit.

Most of us, whether we're Cricut pros or a beginner, have seen the many items for sale at craft shows and in specialty stores. Everything from popular saying and quotes stenciled on wood signs to monogrammed water tumblers and most everything in between.

Some Cricut users have mastered the machine and they can make vinyl letters look as if they were painted onto the wood. The vinyl meshes so well that with the naked eye you won't be able to find a spot to lift one of the vinyl letters. That's how realistic it can look. And, most vinyls are weather-resistant. That means you can make all kinds of awesome things for outside as well as inside.

Cricut has come so far since the days of die-cutting for scrapbooking, and although scrapbooking is still popular, you don't see as many sheets of stickers in stores, and in some stores, the scrapbooking section has shrunk since Cricut has become so much more than your scrapbooking partner.

And that's not to say scrapbooking isn't fun, but it is to say that ideas are endless and you can make almost anything you can think of.

Best of all, many Cricut models are Bluetooth enabled, making it easy to communicate with your other devices.

One of the nice features of a Cricut machine is that it doesn't take up too much space. It's about the size of a home printer; however, you will most likely want a large workspace for your tools and materials.

What machine should I buy?

Before we get started on how to use the Design Space feature, let's review the types of machines available. There are many to choose from and for first-time buyers, it can be daunting to select the right one. We'll focus on the more recent models. Your budget and how you intend to use the machine are big factors; however, you'll find most Cricut machines are around the same price with the exception of the Cuttlebug Machine.

This is a small, portable hand-crank machine that has a maximum cutting width of six inches. It only works with dies and embossing folders; however, it's perfect for those who are looking for a machine they can use for scrapbooking and card making.

The hand-crank machine has been a staple in the Cricut family and you can usually find a new one for under $100. A used hand-crank can be far less money. If it's in good condition and that's what you want, you can sometimes find them for as low as $25 at garage sales and garage sale sites.

This year, a new model was released called The Cricut Maker™. This has all the bells and whistles to do most anything. It has the capability of cutting more materials than any previous models and the company boasts its fast, precise cutting.

The Cricut Maker can be used with your own images, which is a plus for those who prefer to use their own or don't want to buy a subscription or pay for individual images. It allows you to personalize your items and make your own statement. You can make personalized cards, signs, and anything your heart desires. The ability to personalize your items with multiple lines and fonts broadens your horizon, and if you make products to sell, you can offer personalization.

The Cricut Maker is supposed to be better than the Cricut Explore Air 2, and is considered the top-of-the-line. The Explore is promoted as being easier to use than the Maker. It works with paper, vinyl and cardstock, which is a plus.

Of course, you'll need the tools of the trade and these are sold in what are called "Bundles." There are many bundles available, and you can purchase them alone or with your machine, with the exception of the hand-crank model.

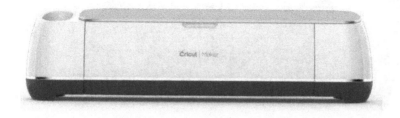

A bundle includes the machine and a set of accessories. The bundles vary; however, many include printable sticker paper, cardstock, trimmers and cutting tools, pens, and usually free project ideas. Each model comes with a different bundle.

Once you have your machine, you'll need dies. There are two options–Cricut Access and Cricut Design Space.

The two are often confused, so let's touch briefly on the differences.

Cricut Access

When you purchased your Cricut, you may have been offered a 30-day free trial for Cricut Access.

Cricut Access is a subscription-based program that gives you access to images and fonts without an extra charge, provided your subscription is up-to-date. The images and fonts are only available to those with an active subscription and if you don't pay, you'll no longer have access. The subscription is use-only; it does not allow you to keep the images and fonts. That is a common misconception.

How much you use your machine will determine if it's worth it for you to subscribe. If you're a heavy user and make a lot of different items, then a monthly or annual subscription might be right for you. This is a good choice if you're a crafter making a variety of items to sell.

Country stores and those selling folk art sometimes can't keep up with the demand for wooden or chalkboard signs. Sayings and inspirational quotes are popular right now, and if you're one of the lucky ones profiting from the craze, you'll get your money's worth from the subscription.

If you've decided a subscription is the way to go, there are three options:

The monthly basic plan currently costs $9.99 per month and is billed monthly. The annual plan is $7.99 per month with a one-time annual billing of $95.88. The premium plan costs $119.88 annually.

Of course, you might be able to find a coupon code online and save a few dollars, and the premium subscription will give you 50% off on images and fonts not included in the basic subscription.

Cricut Access is used with Design Space.

Design Space

Cricut Design Space is an app that is used with the Cricut Explore and Cricut Maker™ machines. What makes Design Space unique is that it lets you wirelessly cut your designs.

You can get Cricut Design Space from the Apple™ store as a free download.

The app offers you access to Make It Now™ projects and fonts in the Cricut® Image Library along with thousands of images, according to Apple's promo.

Apple describes Cricut Design Space as an app offering the following features:

Design and cut DIY projects with Cricut Explore and Cricut Maker cutting machines

Choose from over 50,000 images, fonts, and projects in the Cricut Image Library—or use your own images and fonts for free

Upload and clean up your own images

Design and cut without an Internet connection using fonts and images downloaded to your device

Cut quick and easy predesigned Make It Now™ projects

Make home and party décor, cards, and invitations, scrapbooking, fashion, jewelry, kids' crafts, and more

Cut a wide variety of materials including paper, vinyl, iron-on, cardstock, poster board, fabric—even thicker materials like leather

Use the built-in camera on your device to position, and visualize your projects on a real-life background

Sign in with your Cricut ID to access your images and projects and for easy checkout when making purchases on Cricut.com or in Design Space

Bluetooth® wireless capability By now, you've probably downloaded an app from the Apple Store, so we'll bypass instructions as to how to do so. If you've never done it before, use the Apple Store help menu and it'll be self-explanatory.

With these explanations behind us, let's begin taking the steps you'll need to successfully use Cricut Design Space.

Now that we've been introduced, let's get started!

If you are a Windows user, Design Space is typically installed on your PC through the new machine setup process, but you can manually install it through the steps below:

Open an internet browser and go to design.cricut.com. When the page has loaded, sign in with your Cricut ID, or create one if you don't have one.

Once signed in, select the New Project tile. You will receive a prompt to download and install the Design Space plugin. Select Download. Watch for the screen to change as the plugin file is downloaded.

When the file is downloaded, select the file or find it in your Downloads folder to Open or Run it. If you receive a message asking if you want to allow this app to make changes to your device, select Yes. You may be required to enter your computer's "Admin" password to continue.

When you receive a notice that the Setup wizard is ready to begin installing Cricut Design Space, select Next to begin the installation.

The setup wizard will display the installation progress and notify you when the installation is complete. Select Finish. Now you can begin using Design Space.

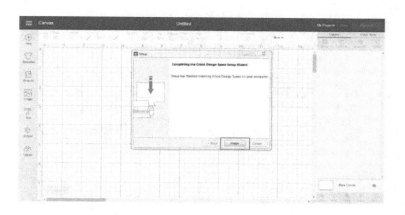

20

Chapter 1
Project Ideas

Projects and Ideas With Vinyl

Vinyl is one of the most common supplies to use with Cricut machines, no matter which one you have. The Cricut Explore One, Cricut Explore Air 2, and Cricut Maker all easily cut through vinyl. The Cricut EasyPress makes using heat transfer vinyl incredibly easy. Vinyl can serve as the design itself, a removable sticker, or a stencil. These ten projects were chosen to cover a wide range of methods and different types of vinyl. Feel free to follow the instructions exactly, or change the types of materials listed.

There are several different types of vinyl. Most of the projects specify which vinyl to use, but you could use different ones depending on the use of the object. The four basic categories that all vinyl falls under are permanent, removable, iron-on (or heat transfer vinyl), and window cling. Permanent vinyl is designed to last and is good for outdoor projects, projects that are going to get a lot of handling, and projects you'll want to be able to wash.

Removable vinyl is just that. It's adhesive and can be

removed again. It's not suited for outdoor use or heavy handling. It's often used for stencils or temporary stickers. A heat transfer vinyl transfers to a surface using heat and pressure from something like an iron or a Cricut EasyPress. Finally, window cling is another type of vinyl with temporary use, but it's not actually adhesive. It uses static to adhere to glass or other very smooth surfaces.

Cricut offers a wide variety of vinyl types. They have different colors and patterns, shimmer, glitter, holographic, glossy, dry erase, chalkboard, printable, and stencil vinyl. For the most part, whatever you get will come down to personal preference and what you want to use it for. However, some may only be available in permanent, temporary, or is otherwise limited. The best thing to do is search by the usage first, then choose a color and finish from that listing. Vinyl transfer tape is a crucial component no matter what type of vinyl you are using. If you are shopping Cricut brand, they offer regular and Strong Grip transfer tape. The Strong Grip is for tougher vinyl, such as glitter. If you are buying different brands of vinyl, they will often come with transfer tape to use with them. If they don't, you should be able to find it separately at the same store.

Project 01: Treasure Chest Jewelry Box

Turn a simple wooden box into a treasure chest! This is a cute project for yourself or your child. Choose the type of wooden box you like best. You can find one with flat or rounded lids and in all different sizes.

You could get one that's already in the color you like, a light color to stain or paint yourself, or even an older box that looks like it could be a treasure chest.

White vinyl is a good basic that will show up on any wood, but you could change the color depending on how you want your box to look. Scale this up to create a toy or storage box. You can use the Cricut Explore One, Cricut Explore Air 2, or Cricut Maker for this project.

Supplies Needed

- Plain wooden box with lid
- White vinyl
- Vinyl transfer tape
- Cutting mat
- Weeding tool or pick
- Small blade

Instructions

1. Open Cricut Design Space and create a new project.

2. Select the "Image" button in the lower left-hand corner and search for "keyhole."

3. Click your favorite keyhole design and click "Insert."

4. Select the "Text" button in the lower left-hand corner.

5. Choose your favorite font and type "Treasure."

6. Place your vinyl on the cutting mat.

7. Send the design to your Cricut.

8. Use a weeding tool or pick to remove the excess vinyl from the design.

9. Apply separate pieces of transfer tape to the keyhole and the word.

10. Remove the paper backing from the tape on the keyhole.

11. Place the keyhole where the lid and box meet so that half is on the lid and half is on the box.

12. Rub the tape to transfer the vinyl to the wood, making sure there are no bubbles. Carefully peel the tape away.

13. Use a sharp blade to cut the keyhole design in half so that the box can open.

14. Transfer the word to the front of the box using the same method.

15. Optional: Add details with paint or markers to make the box look more like a treasure chest. Add wood grain, barnacles, seashells, or pearls.

16. Store your jewelry in your new treasure chest!

Project 02: Motivational Water Bottle

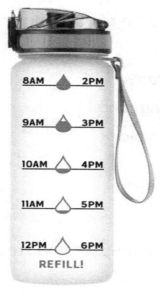

Everyone needs a motivational boost to keep their workouts going. Turn a boring water bottle into your personal cheerleader! Choose the type of water bottle that you like the best, whether it's a plastic, glass, or metal one. This could also work on a reusable tumbler if you prefer to have a straw. The glitter vinyl will give a fun accent to your necessary hydration, but you can change it to a regular color if you want to be a bit less flashy. Use one of the suggested quotes or one of your own. The important thing is that it motivates you to keep moving! You can use the Cricut Explore One, Cricut Explore Air 2, or Cricut Maker for this project.

Supplies Needed

- Sturdy water bottle of your choice
- Glitter vinyl
- Vinyl transfer tape
- Light grip cutting mat
- Weeding tool or pick

Instructions

1. Open Cricut Design Space and create a new project.

2. Measure the space on your water bottle where you want the text, and create a box that size.

3. Select the "Text" button in the lower left-hand corner.

4. Choose your favorite font, and type the motivational quote you like best.

a. I sweat glitter

b. Sweat is magic

c. I don't sweat, I sparkle

5. Place your vinyl on the cutting mat.

6. Send the design to your Cricut.

7. Use a weeding tool or pick to remove the excess vinyl from the text.

8. Apply transfer tape to the quote.

9. Remove the paper backing from the tape.

10. Place the quote where you want it on the water bottle.

11. Rub the tape to transfer the vinyl to the bottle, making sure there are no bubbles. Carefully peel the tape away.

12. Bring your new water bottle to the gym for motivation and hydration!

Project 03: Customized Makeup Bag

Bathroom counter a mess from all your makeup? Make yourself a cute bag to store it in! This can be any size bag or pouch you'd like, from one that holds a few items to a train case. The only requirement is enough blank space for the design. Pink and purple create a classic, feminine look, but you can use whatever color combination suits you best. This is the first project using heat transfer vinyl, so you'll need a Cricut EasyPress or iron to transfer the design onto the bag. You can use the Cricut Explore One, Cricut Explore Air 2, or Cricut Maker for this project.

Supplies Needed

- Pink fabric makeup bag

- Purple heat transfer vinyl

- Cricut EasyPress or iron

- Cutting mat

- Weeding tool or pick

- Keychain or charm of your choice

Instructions

1. Open Cricut Design Space and create a new project.

2. Measure the space on your makeup bag where you want the design, and create a box that size.

3. Select the "Image" button in the lower left-hand corner and search

"monogram."

4. Choose your favorite monogram and click "Insert."
5. Place your vinyl on the cutting mat.

6. Send the design to your Cricut.

7. Use a weeding tool or pick to remove the excess vinyl from the design.

8. Place the design on the bag with the plastic side up.

9. Carefully iron on the design.

10. After cooling, peel away the plastic by rolling it.

11. Hang your charm or keychain off the zipper.

12. Stash your makeup in your customized bag!

Project 04: Perpetual Calendar

Woodblock calendars are a cute addition to any décor. Many teachers use them on their desks, or they fit in anywhere in your home. You can find unfinished block calendars online or at most craft stores. They'll usually have two wooden cubes for the numbers, two longer blocks for the months, and a stand to hold them. Painting the wood will give you the color of your choice, but you could also stain it or look around for calendars made of different types of wood. You can use the Cricut Explore One, Cricut Explore Air 2, or Cricut Maker for this project.

Supplies Needed

- Unfinished woodblock calendar

- Acrylic paint in color(s) of your choosing.

- Vinyl color(s) of your choosing

- Vinyl transfer tape

- Cutting mat

- Weeding tool or pick

- Mod Podge

Instructions

1. Paint the woodblock calendar in the colors you'd like and set aside to dry.

2. Open Cricut Design Space, and create a new project.

3. Create a square the correct size for the four blocks.

4. Select the "Text" button in the lower left-hand corner.

5. Choose your favorite font, and type the following numbers as well as all of the months: 0, 0, 1, 1, 2, 2, 3, 4, 5, 6, 7, 8

6. Place your vinyl on the cutting mat.

7. Send the design to your Cricut.

8. Use a weeding tool or pick to remove the excess vinyl from the text.

9. Apply transfer tape to each separate number and the months.

10. Remove the paper backing from the tape, and apply the numbers as follows.

➤ 0 and 5 on the top and bottom of the first block

➤ 1, 2, 3, 4 around the sides of the first block

➤ 0 and 8 on the top and bottom of the second block

> 1, 2, 6, 7 around the sides of the second block

11. Remove the paper backing from the tape on the months, and apply them to the long blocks, the first six months on one and the second six months on the other.

12. Rub the tape to transfer the vinyl to the wood, making sure there are no bubbles. Carefully peel the tape away.

13. Seal everything with a coat of Mod Podge.

14. Arrange your calendar to display today's date, and enjoy it year after year!

Project 05: Wooden Gift Tags

Dress up your gifts with special wooden tags! Balsa wood is light and easy to cut. The wood tags with gold names will give all of your gifts a shabby chic charm. Change up the color of the vinyl as you see fit; you can even use different colors for different gift recipients. People will be able to keep these tags and use them for something else, as well. An alternative to balsa wood is chipboard, though it won't have the same look. The Cricut Maker is the best choice for this project, though the Cricut Explore One and Cricut Explore Air 2 can get by using the Deep Cut Blade.

Supplies Needed

- Balsa wood

- Gold vinyl

- Vinyl transfer tape

- Cutting mat

- Weeding tool or pick

Instructions

1. Secure your small balsa wood pieces to the cutting mat, then tape the edges with masking tape for additional strength.

2. Open Cricut Design Space and create a new project.

3. Select the shape you would like for your tags and set the Cricut to cut wood, then send the design to the Cricut.

4. Remove your wood tags from the Cricut and remove any excess wood.

5. In Cricut Design Space, select the "Text" button in

the lower left-hand corner.

6. Choose your favorite font, and type the names you want to place on your gift tags.

7. Place your vinyl on the cutting mat.

8. Send the design to your Cricut.

9. Use a weeding tool or pick to remove the excess vinyl from the text.

10. Apply transfer tape to the quote.

11. Remove the paper backing from the tape.

12. Place the names on the wood tags.

13. Rub the tape to transfer the vinyl to the wood, making sure there are no bubbles. Carefully peel the tape away.

14. Thread twine or string through the holes, and decorate your gifts!

Project 06: Pet Mug

Show your love for your pet every morning when you have your coffee! A cute silhouette of a cat or dog with some paw prints is a simple but classy design. You're not limited to those two animals, either. Use a bird with bird footprints, a fish with water drops, or whatever pet you might have! You can add your pet's name or a quote to the design as well. You have the freedom here to arrange the aspects of the design however you'd like. You could put the animal in the center surrounded by the paw prints, scatter the prints all around the mug, place the animal next to its name and paw prints along the top, or whatever else you can imagine. Think of this as a tribute to your favorite pet or dedication to your favorite animal, and decorate accordingly. You can use the Cricut Explore One, Cricut Explore Air 2, or Cricut Maker for this project.

Supplies Needed

- Plain white mug

- Glitter vinyl

- Vinyl transfer tape

- Cutting mat

- Weeding tool or pick

Instructions

1. Open Cricut Design Space and create a new project.

2. Select the "Image" button in the lower left-hand corner and search for "cat," "dog," or any other pet of your choice.

3. Choose your favorite image and click "Insert."

4. Search images again for paw prints, and insert into your design.

5. Arrange the pet and paw prints how you'd like them on the mug.

6. Place your vinyl on the cutting mat.

7. Send the design to your Cricut.

8. Use a weeding tool or pick to remove the excess vinyl from the design.

9. Apply transfer tape to the design.

10. Remove the paper backing, and apply the design to the mug.

11. Rub the tape to transfer the vinyl to the mug, making sure there are no bubbles. Carefully peel the tape away.

12. Enjoy your custom pet mug!

Project 07: Organized Toy Bins

How much of a mess is your kids' room? We already know the answer to that. Grab some plastic bins and label them with different toy categories, and teach your child to sort! You can use the type of bins that suit your child or their room best. Many people like to use the ones that look like giant buckets with handles on the sides. There are also more simple square ones. You could even use cheaper laundry baskets or plastic totes with or without the lids. Once your child is old enough to read the labels, it will be easier for them to put away toys and find them again to play. You can add images to the designs as well—whatever will make your child like them best! You can use the Cricut Explore One, Cricut Explore Air 2, or Cricut Maker for this project.

Supplies Needed

Plastic toy bins in colors of your choice

- White vinyl

- Vinyl transfer tape

- Cutting mat

- Weeding tool or pick

Instructions

1. Open Cricut Design Space and create a new project.

2. Select the "Text" button in the lower left-hand corner.

3. Choose your favorite font and type the labels for each toy bin. See below for some possibilities.

a. Legos

b. Dolls

c. Cars

d. Stuffed animals

e. Outside Toys

4. Place your vinyl on the cutting mat.

5. Send the design to your Cricut.

6. Use a weeding tool or pick to remove the excess vinyl from the text.

7. Apply transfer tape to the words.

8. Remove the paper backing and apply the design to the bin.

9. Rub the tape to transfer the vinyl to the bin, making sure there are no bubbles. Carefully peel the tape away.

10. Organize your kid's toys in your new bins!

Project 08: Froggy Rain Gear

Kids love to play outside in the rain. It can be hard to get them to dress properly for it, though. Decorate a raincoat and rain boots with a cute froggy design that will have them asking to wear them! A simple raincoat and boots that you can find at any store for a reasonable price become custom pieces with this project. The outdoor vinyl is made to withstand the elements and last for ages. You can customize this even more by adding your child's name or change up the theme completely with different images. You can use the Cricut Explore One, Cricut Explore Air 2, or Cricut Maker for this project.

Supplies Needed

- Matching green raincoat and rain boots

- White outdoor vinyl

- Vinyl transfer tape

- Cutting mat

- Weeding tool or pick

Instructions

1. Open Cricut Design Space and create a new project.

2. Select the "Image" button in the lower left-hand corner and search for "frog."

3. Choose your favorite frog and click "Insert."

4. Copy the frog and resize. You will need three frogs, a larger one for the coat and two smaller ones for each boot.

5. Place your vinyl on the cutting mat.

6. Send the design to your Cricut.

7. Use a weeding tool or pick to remove the excess vinyl from the design.

8. Apply transfer tape to the design.

9. Remove the paper backing and apply the design to the coat or boot.

10. Rub the tape to transfer the vinyl to the rain gear, making sure there are no bubbles. Carefully peel the tape away.

11. Dress your kid up to play in the rain!

Project 09: Snowy Wreath

Wreaths are a popular decoration year-round. This one is perfect for winter. You can buy premade grapevine wreaths at almost any store, or you can get really crafty and assemble one yourself. The berry stems can be found in the floral sections of craft stores. Silver will fit the snowy theme well, but you could also use red for a holiday-themed look or an entirely different color.

You can also change up the whole project to theme it toward your winter holiday of choice. You can use the Cricut Explore One, Cricut Explore Air 2, or Cricut Maker for this project.

Supplies Needed

- Grapevine wreath

- Silver berry stems

- Spray adhesive

- Silver and white glitter

- Piece of wood to fit across the center of the wreath Wood stain, if desired

- Drill and a small bit

- Twine

- White vinyl

- Vinyl transfer tape

- Cutting mat

- Weeding tool or pick

Instructions

1. Thread the silver berry stems throughout the grapevine wreath.

2. Use the spray adhesive and glitter to create patches of "snow" on the wreath.

3. If you want to stain your wood, do so now and set it aside to dry.

4. Open Cricut Design Space and create a new project.

5. Select the "Text" button in the lower left-hand corner.

6. Choose your favorite font and type, "Let it snow."

7. Place your vinyl on the cutting mat.

8. Send the design to your Cricut.

9. Use a weeding tool or pick to remove the excess vinyl from the text.

10. Apply transfer tape to the words.

11. Remove the paper backing and apply the design to the wood piece.

12. Rub the tape to transfer the vinyl to the wood, making sure there are no bubbles. Carefully peel the tape away.

13. Drill two small holes in the corner of the wood and thread the twine through.

14. Hang your wreath and sign for the winter season!

Project 10: Antiqued Kitchen Sign

Aged wooden signs are easy but effective décor, and they are very chic right now. You can create one of your own with little effort! Spray paint is easy to use. It would create the aged look by not laying down an even coat. Use it in short, sweeping bursts to avoid getting too much in one spot. You can change up the colors if you'd like, or add another coat to customize the look. There are also different stains and finishes you can use. Take a look at crackle paint for a really aged look. Use the vinyl to spell out one of the phrases below, or use one of your own that represents your home best. You can use the Cricut Explore One, Cricut Explore Air 2, or Cricut Maker for this project.

Supplies Needed

- Wooden sign of the desired size
- Black and white spray paint
- Vinyl
- Vinyl transfer tape
- Cutting mat
- Weeding tool or pick

Instructions

1. Paint the sign black and set it aside to dry.

2. Open Cricut Design Space and create a new project.

3. Select the "Text" button in the lower left-hand corner.

4. Choose your favorite font and type a phrase for your kitchen sign.

See below for some possibilities.

➢ Eat Here

➢ Marketplace

➢ Family

➢ Gather Here

➢ Diner

5. Place your vinyl on the cutting mat.

6. Send the design to your Cricut.

7. Use a weeding tool or pick to remove the excess vinyl from the text.

8. Apply transfer tape to the words.

9. Remove the paper backing and apply the design to the sign.

10. Rub the tape to transfer the vinyl to the wood, making sure there are no bubbles. Carefully peel the tape away.

11. Use white spray paint on the whole sign. Do so messily, leaving some spots of black for the aged appearance. Set aside to dry.

12. After drying, peel away the vinyl letters.

13. Hang your sign and enjoy!

Chapter 2
Projects and Ideas With Paper

After vinyl, the paper is incredibly popular for Cricut projects. It's definitely the cheapest and easiest to find among all the materials. Cardstock is usually the first choice, as it's sturdy and can handle a lot of folding, cutting, and art supplies. There are hundreds of thousands of varieties of paper, though, and you can experiment to see what you like best. The types of paper listed for each project is merely a suggestion. Paper also has the advantage of working well in every Cricut machine.

With paper, in particular, you'll want to make sure your blade is sharp and clean. Anything out of the ordinary will tear the paper. Dull blades are the biggest culprit when you find tears in your paper. Make sure you're using the appropriate blade for the weight of the paper as well. Some thicker papers might just need a second pass rather than a sharper blade. It's good to have some spare paper that you can do test runs with.

If you're using a new cutting mat, you'll need to condition it before you put your paper on it. New mats are very sticky, and you won't be able to get the paper off again without tearing it. Conditioning is quick and easy, though.

Simply touch the mat with your hands. The oils on your skin will decrease the stickiness without damaging your mat. Touch repeatedly until mat feels less sticky, and make sure to get all of the edges and corners. Test the mat with some scrap paper before using it for your project.

Paper can be found at just about any store. However, some specialty stores and websites will actually give you a cheat sheet on how to cut their different papers with different cutting machines. You might find a list of all of their papers and which blades and settings to use for them. Some will even offer instructions for creating a custom material for specific papers. Check out the help section of specialty paper websites to see if they have this.

The Cricut machines don't just cut paper; they can also write and draw. Cricut offers a wide selection of different pens, and there are other brands that will fit in the machine as well. A couple of the following projects take advantage of this feature, but you can incorporate it into the others as well. You can draw or write anything on any of your patterns. With the Cricut Explore One and Cricut Explore Air 2, you'll need to swap out pens if you want to change colors. The Cricut Maker has two tool carriages, so you can do at least two colors at once without swapping.

Project 11: Paper Bouquet

Flowers are nice, but it doesn't take long for them to wilt. How about some paper ones instead? They'll last you forever! Use this bouquet as décor in your home or for an event. Budget-conscious brides can even carry this down the aisle instead of an expensive floral arrangement! You will find plenty of templates in the Cricut Design Space for different flowers. You can also search online for more, or you can try your hand at making your own. A bouquet can be made up of one type of flower, the same flower in different colors, a variety of flowers, or a variety of flowers, all in the same color. It depends on the look and feel that you are going for, so use whatever method sounds best to you. You can use plain cardstock, patterned cardstock, or use watercolor to create a color gradient you love. For the stems, pipe cleaners are easier to work with and can be covered with tissue paper or something similar. Or, it can be left visible for a crafty look. The floral wire will give a more realistic look, but it's thinner and takes some work. You can use the Cricut Explore One, Cricut Explore Air 2, or Cricut Maker for this project.

Supplies Needed

- Cardstock

- Glue gun

- Lightstick cutting mat

- Weeding tool or pick

- Green pipe cleaners or floral wire

Instructions

1. Open Cricut Design Space and create a new project.

2. Select the "Image" button in the lower left-hand corner and search for "paper flowers."

3. Select the image with several flower pieces and click "Insert."

4. Copy the flowers and resize for variety in your bouquet.

5. Place your cardstock on the cutting mat.

6. Send the design to your Cricut.

7. Remove the outer edge of the paper, leaving the flowers on the mat.

8. Use your weeding tool or carefully pick to remove the flowers from the mat.

9. Glue the flower pieces together in the centers, with the largest petals at the bottom.

10. Bend or curl petals as desired to create multiple looks.

11. Glue the flowers to the ends of the pipe cleaners or sections of floral wire.

12. Gather your flowers together in a vase or wrap them with tissue paper.

13. Enjoy your beautiful bouquet!

Project 12: Leafy Garland

Garlands are an easy way to spruce up any space, and there is an infinite variety of them. Create a unique leafy one to give your home a more naturalistic feel! Feel free to change the colors of the leaves to suit you, whether you stick with green or go a little more unnatural. Tweaking the size of the bundles you make and how close you put them together will change the look of the garland. You can use different types of leaves as well.

Experiment a little bit to see what you like best. Bending the leaves down the center and curling the edges a little will give you a more realistic look, or you can leave them flat for a handmade look. You can use the Cricut Explore One, Cricut Explore Air 2, or Cricut Maker for this project.

Supplies Needed

- Cardstock – 2 or more colors of green, or white to paint yourself Glue gun

- Lightstick cutting mat

- Weeding tool or pick

- Floral wire

- Floral tape

Instructions

1. Open Cricut Design Space and create a new project.

2. Select the "Image" button in the lower left-hand corner and search for "leaf collage."

3. Select the image of leaves and click "Insert."

4. Place your cardstock on the cutting mat.

5. Send the design to your Cricut.

6. Remove the outer edge of the paper, leaving the leaves on the mat.

7. Use a pick or scoring tool to score down the center of each leaf lightly.

8. Use your weeding tool or carefully pick to remove the leaves from the mat.

9. Gently bend each leaf at the score line.

10. Glue the leaves into bunches of two or three.

11. Cut a length of floral wire to your desired garland size, and wrap the ends with floral tape.

12. Attach the leaf bunches to the wire using the floral tape.

13. Continue attaching leaves until you have a garland of the size you want. Bundle lots of leaves for a really full look, or spread them out to be sparser.

14. Create hooks at the ends of the garland with floral wire.

15. Hang your beautiful leaf garland wherever you'd like!

Project 13: Easy Envelope Addressing

Christmas cards are wonderful to send out, but they can take forever to address. Address labels just don't look as personal, though. Use the Cricut pen tool in your machine to "hand letter" your envelopes! You can use this for your batch of holiday cards or even for other cards or letters. This takes advantage of the writing function of your Cricut machine. For the most realistic written look, make sure you select a font in the writing style. It will still write other fonts, but it will only create an outline of them, which is a different look you could go for! Cricut offers a variety of Pen Tools, and there are some other pens that will fit as well. For addressing envelopes, stick to black or another color that is easy to read so that the mail makes it to its destination. You can use the Cricut Explore One, Cricut Explore Air 2, or Cricut Maker for this project.

Supplies Needed

- Envelopes to address

- Cricut Pen Tool

- Lightstick cutting mat

Instructions

1. Open Cricut Design Space and create a new project.

2. Create a box the appropriate size for your envelopes.

3. Select the "Text" button in the lower left-hand corner.

4. Choose one handwriting font for a uniform look or different fonts for each line to mix it up.

5. Type your return address in the upper left-hand corner of the design.

6. Type the "to" address in the center of the design.

7. Insert your Cricut pen into the auxiliary holder of your Cricut, making sure it is secure.

8. Place your cardstock on the cutting mat.

9. Send the design to your Cricut.

10. Remove your envelope and repeat as needed.

11. Send out your "hand-lettered" envelopes!

Project 14: Watercolor Heart Sign

Watercolor designs are very trendy right now and surprisingly easy to make. You don't need any prior artistic experience to make this sign! You can pick up cheap watercolors from almost any store. You certainly don't need expensive ones for this design. Play with different colors and different textures of paper to get exactly what you want. Watercolor paper is designed to handle lots of water, but other thick papers can handle paint as well. Thin papers will warp and buckle when they get wet. For the most unified look, pick out a frame that coordinates with the watercolors you use. You can use the Cricut Explore One, Cricut Explore Air 2, or Cricut Maker for this project.

Supplies Needed

- Watercolor paper
- Watercolor paints and paintbrush
- Glue
- Lightstick cutting mat
- Weeding tool or pick
- Frame

Instructions

1. Paint your watercolor paper in soft gradients. Use a lot of water and gradually blend two or three colors into each other. Set aside to dry.

2. Open Cricut Design Space, and create a new project.

3. Select the "Image" button in the lower left-hand corner and search for "heart."

4. Select the heart of your choice and click "Insert."

5. Place your watercolor paper on the cutting mat.

6. Send the design to your Cricut.

7. Remove the outer edge of the paper, leaving the heart on the mat.

8. Use your weeding tool or carefully pick to remove the heart from the mat.

9. Glue your heart to the center of a blank piece of paper, cut to fit your frame.

10. Place your sign into your frame.

11. Set or hang wherever you need a little color!

Project 15: Patterned Gift Wrap

Wrapping gifts can be fun, but it's even more fun to make them personalized! Using doodle designs creates a cute and handmade look that everyone will love. You can customize the gift for the occasion or even for the person.

Invite kids to color in the outlines for an even more personal touch! You can pick other types of designs as well. This uses the Cricut writing function. If you decide to use different colors, you'll need to switch pens between them. You can use the Cricut Explore One, Cricut Explore Air 2, or Cricut Maker for this project.

Supplies Needed

- White kraft paper

- Cricut Pen Tool in color(s) of your choice

- 12x24 cutting mat

- Weeding tool or pick

Instructions

1. Open Cricut Design Space and create a new project.

2. Select the "Image" button in the lower left-hand corner and search for doodled images appropriate for the gift you're wrapping, for example, "Christmas doodle" or "birthday doodle."

3. Select the images you like and click "Insert."

4. Copy, resize, and rotate the images to create a pattern you like for the size of your wrapping paper.

5. Change the colors of the doodles if desired—leaving them black creates a coloring-book feel, or you can make them in different colors.

6. Place your paper on the cutting mat.

7. Send the design to your Cricut.

8. Remove your wrapping paper from the mat.

9. Wrap your gift in your customized wrapping paper!

Project 16: Birthday Star Cupcake Toppers

Cupcake toppers can be expensive, and often just get tossed aside. Make these cheap but cute ones on your own instead! Your options are limitless, and you can select a theme for any party or occasion. These gold stars are quick and simple to make and will look good no matter whose birthday you are celebrating. Change the colors and shapes as you see fit. You can scale this up to use as a cake topper as well. Keep the same designs in your Cricut Design Space to print more designs to match—a banner, favor bags, food labels, invitations, and more! You can use the Cricut Explore One, Cricut Explore Air 2, or Cricut Maker for this project.

Supplies Needed

- Cardstock – Glittery gold and white
- Glue stick
- Glue gun
- Lightstick cutting mat
- Weeding tool or pick
- Toothpicks

Instructions

1. Open Cricut Design Space and create a new project.

2. Select the "Image" button in the lower left-hand corner and search for "star."

3. Select the star you like best and click "Insert."

4. Place your gold cardstock on the cutting mat.

5. Send the design to your Cricut.

6. In Design Space, select the "Text" button in the lower left-hand corner.

7. Choose your favorite font and type, "Happy birthday!"

8. Place your white cardstock on the cutting mat.

9. Send the design to your Cricut.

10. Remove the outer edge of the paper, leaving the text on the mat.

11. Use your weeding tool or carefully pick to remove the text from the mat.

12. Use the glue stick to attach the text on top of the stars.

13. Use the glue gun to attach toothpicks to the back of each star.

14. Stick your toppers onto your cupcakes!

Project 17: Holiday Gift Card Holders

Gift cards make a wonderful choice for any occasion. They let the gift recipient pick out their own present and receive a great deal of pressure from you! However, it's boring to hand over a gift card in the packaging that it was in when you pulled it from the shelf. Instead, make this cute cardholder. It can double as a card if you choose to write a message inside! This project takes advantage of a premade template in Cricut Design Space. It provides all of the pieces you need, and you can follow the following instructions to assemble it. Try cutting the different pieces out of different colors or patterns of paper for some variety. You can use the Cricut Explore One, Cricut Explore Air 2, or Cricut Maker for this project.

Supplies Needed

- Holiday-themed scrapbook paper

- Cricut Scoring Stylus

- Light grip cutting mat

- Weeding tool or pick

- Glue stick

- Ribbon, twine, or string to match your paper

Instructions

1. Open Cricut Design Space and create a new project.

2. Select the "Image" button in the lower left-hand corner and search for "gift card."

3. Select the gift cardholder template and click "Insert."

4. Insert the scoring stylus into the Cricut, making sure it is secure.

5. Place your paper on the cutting mat.

6. Send the design to your Cricut.

7. Use the weeding tool or carefully pick to remove the template from the mat.

8. Bend the large outer piece and the inner cardholder where they have been scored.

9. Bend the three tabs on the inner cardholder inward and the one tab on the other side outward.

10. Apply glue to the three tabs and attach.

11. Glue the inner cardholder to the large outer piece with the outward-facing tab.

12. Glue two decorative pieces to the inside and two to the outside.

13. Place the gift card in the holder and tie closed with ribbon, twine, or string.

14. Present your gift card to the recipient!

Chapter 3
Projects and Ideas With Fabric

Projects and Ideas With Fabric Using fabric opens the door to an infinite number of Cricut projects. Whether you like to sew or plan on gluing fabric to things, your machine can cut it for you first. You can revisit the use of heat transfer vinyl as well for further customization. The projects in this chapter range from simple to complex, but you can still tweak any of them for your own purposes. The Cricut Maker is going to be the best machine for most of these projects. The Cricut Explore One and Cricut Explore Air 2 can cut backed fabrics, but the rotary blade on the Maker will be able to cut precisely any fabric without tearing. It is also more powerful, and it can get through thicker and more durable fabrics.

If you have a Cricut Explore One or Cricut Explore Air 2, you will need to bond any fabric you want to cut. The rotary blade in the Cricut Maker can cut any fabric without it needing to be bonded. You may be able to use bonded fabrics for some of these projects, but others will require the rotary blade. If you plan to do a lot of work with fabric, it is worth considering an upgrade to the Cricut Maker.

For fabric, you will be using the pink Fabric Grip mat. The fabric will go right side down on the mat—this is the way the Cricut Maker expects it to be, and it cuts the patterns accordingly. If you have the Cricut Washable Fabric Pen, it can make markings before cutting your patterns. The marker will later come out in the wash. A pair of broad tip tweezers will help you pull the fabric off your mat after cutting. Be gentle when you do this so that you don't stretch your fabric.

The Fabric Grip mat works a little different from the other Cricut cutting mats. The adhesive on it is specially formulated for holding the fabric. It has also been made durable enough to stand up to the additional pressure the Cricut Maker applies. Use a brayer to roll the fabric onto the mat and tweezers to remove it so that the oils from your hands don't damage the adhesive. Never clean your Fabric Grip mat. Don't use the scraper on it or run water on it. It may look messy with threads and lint stuck to it, but the fabric will still stick, and the machine will cut through just fine. If you really feel the need to get some of the bigger debris off, you can use the tweezers and dab at it with Strong Grip transfer tape.

Cricut offers printable fabric. You can use your inkjet printer to print designs

on this fabric. You can find designs or create your own in Cricut Design Space. This lets you create custom details for your fabric projects.

Experiment and see what you can create and print on fabric and how you can use this to add to your projects.

Test cuts are very important with fabric. Every type of fabric cuts differently, and sometimes, even different pieces among the same type will be different.

Even though the machine automatically sets the pressure based on the material you've selected, feel free to adjust it if necessary. If you're working with fabric that frays easily, it can help to increase the pressure of the blade.

However, make those test cuts before adjusting anything. Your Maker will probably surprise you at first with how intelligent it is when it comes to cutting fabric.

Project 18: Tassels

Tassels have almost endless uses. These are incredibly easy to make and can be customized to fit whatever purpose you want. Add them to the edges of pillows or blankets, hang them from a string to make a banner, use one as a keychain or zipper pull, and a million other things! You can also try making these with leather or faux leather for a classier look. Tassels are cute on just about everything. For best results, use your Cricut Maker for this project.

Supplies Needed

- 12" x 18" fabric rectangles

- Fabric mat

- Glue gun

Instructions

1. Open Cricut Design Space and create a new project.

2. Select the "Image" button in the lower left-hand corner and search "tassel."

3. Select the image of a rectangle with lines on each side and click "Insert."

4. Place the fabric on the cutting mat.

5. Send the design to the Cricut.

6. Remove the fabric from the mat, saving the extra square.

7. Place the fabric face down and begin rolling tightly, starting on the uncut side. Untangle the fringe as needed.

8. Use some of the scrap fabric and a hot glue gun to secure the tassel at the top.

9. Decorate whatever you want with your new tassels!

Project 19: Monogrammed Drawstring Bag

Drawstring bags are quick and easy to use. They're just as easy to make! This includes steps for sewing the pieces together, but you could even use fabric glue if you're not great with a needle and thread. You can keep these bags handy for every member of your family to grab and go as needed. You can tell them apart with the monograms, or use a different design on each one to customize them to a certain use or just decorate it. You can even use these as gift bags! This project uses heat transfer vinyl for the designs, so you'll need your Cricut EasyPress or iron. For best results, use your Cricut Maker for this project.

Supplies Needed

- Two matching rectangles of fabric
- Needle and thread
- Ribbon
- Heat transfer vinyl
- Cricut EasyPress or iron
- Cutting mat
- Weeding tool or pick

Instructions

1. Open Cricut Design Space and create a new project.

2. Select the "Image" button in the lower left-hand corner and search "monogram."

3. Select the monogram of your choice and click "Insert."

4. Place the iron-on material shiny liner side down on the cutting mat.

5. Send the design to the Cricut.

6. Use the weeding tool or pick to remove excess material.

7. Remove the monogram from the mat.

8. Center the monogram on your fabric, then move it a couple of inches down so that it won't be folded up when the ribbon is drawn.

9. Iron the design onto the fabric.

10. Place the two rectangles together, with the outer side of the fabric facing inward.

11. Sew around the edges, leaving a seam allowance.

12. Leave the top open and stop a couple of inches down from the top.

13. Fold the top of the bag down until you reach your stitches.

14. Sew along the bottom of the folded edge, leaving the sides open.

15. Turn the bag right side out.

16. Thread the ribbon through the loop around the top of the bag.

17. Use your new drawstring bag to carry what you need

Project 20: Paw Print Socks

Socks are the ultimate cozy item. No warm pajamas are complete without a pair! Add a cute, hidden accent to the bottom of your or your child's socks with little paw prints. Show off your love for your pet or animals, in general, every time you cuddle up! You can do this with almost any small design or even use text to add a quote to the bottom of your feet. You can use any type of socks you find comfortable. For the easiest read, make sure the sock color and vinyl color contrast. Or, make them in the same color for a hidden design! The shine of the vinyl will stand out from the cloth in certain lights.

Since this uses heat transfer vinyl, you'll need your Cricut EasyPress or iron.

You can use the Cricut Explore One, Cricut Air 2, or Cricut Maker for this project.

Supplies Needed

- Socks
- Heat transfer vinyl
- Cutting mat
- Scrap cardboard
- Weeding tool or pick
- Cricut EasyPress or iron

Instructions

1. Open Cricut Design Space and create a new project.

2. Select the "Image" button in the lower left-hand corner and search

"paw prints."

3. Select the paw prints of your choice and click "Insert."

4. Place the iron-on material on the mat.

5. Send the design to the Cricut.

6. Use the weeding tool or pick to remove excess material.

7. Remove the material from the mat.

8. Fit the scrap cardboard inside of the socks.

9. Place the iron-on material on the bottom of the

socks.

10. Use the EasyPress to adhere it to the iron-on material.

11. After cooling, remove the cardboard from the socks.

12. Wear your cute paw print socks!

Project 21: Night Sky Pillow

Night Sky Pillow The night sky is a beautiful thing, and you will love having a piece of it on a cozy pillow. Customize this with the stars you love most, or add constellations, planets, galaxies, and more! Adults and children alike can enjoy these lovely pillows. A sewing machine will make this project a breeze to put together, or you can use a needle and thread. If you're not great at sewing, use fabric glue to close the pillow. Choose a soft fabric that you love so that you can cuddle up with this pillow. You will need your Cricut EasyPress or iron to attach the heat transfer vinyl. You can use the Cricut Explore One, Cricut Explore Air 2, or Cricut Maker for this project.

Supplies Needed

- Black, dark blue, or dark purple fabric

- Heat transfer vinyl in gold or silver

- Cutting mat

- Polyester batting

- Weeding tool or pick

- Cricut EasyPress

Instructions

1. Decide the shape you want for your pillow, and cut two matching shapes out of the fabric.

2. Open Cricut Design Space and create a new project.

3. Select the "Image" button in the lower left-hand corner and search

"stars."

4. Select the stars of your choice and click "Insert."

5. Place the iron-on material on the mat.

6. Send the design to the Cricut.

7. Use the weeding tool or pick to remove excess material.

8. Remove the material from the mat.

9. Place the iron-on material on the fabric.

10. Use the EasyPress to adhere it to the iron-on material.

11. Sew the two fabric pieces together, leaving allowance for a seam and a small space open.

12. Fill the pillow with polyester batting through the small open space.

13. Sew the pillow shut.

14. Cuddle up to your starry pillow!

Project 22: Clutch Purse

Clutches are an incredibly useful thing to have around. It is smaller than a regular purse yet big enough to hold what you need, and you can use them for any occasion. Create a few of these in different colors and patterns to match different outfits! This clutch is inspired by a project that Cricut has in the Design Space. It is the most advanced of the fabric projects in this book, and it uses the most sewing. For the best results, use the Cricut Maker for this project.

Supplies Needed

- Two fabrics, one for the exterior and one for the interior Fusible fleece

- Fabric cutting mat

- D-ring

- Sew-on snap

- Lace

- Zipper

- Sewing machine

- Fabric scissors

- Keychain or charm of your choice

Instructions

1. Open Cricut Design Space and create a new project.

2. Select the "Image" button in the lower left-hand corner and search for "essential wallet."

3. Select the essential wallet template and click "Insert."

4. Place the fabric on the mat.

5. Send the design to the Cricut.

6. Remove the fabric from the mat.

7. Attach the fusible fleecing to the wrong side of the exterior fabric.

8. Attach lace to the edges of the exterior fabric.

9. Assemble the D-ring strap.

10. Place the D-ring onto the strap and sew into place.

11. Fold the pocket pieces wrong side out over the top of the zipper, and sew it into place.

12. Fold the pocket's wrong side in and sew the sides.

13. Sew the snap onto the pocket.

14. Lay the pocket on the right side of the main fabric

lining so that the corners of the pocket's bottom are behind the curved edges of the lining fabric. Sew the lining piece to the zipper tape.

15. Fold the lining behind the pocket and iron in place.

16. Sew on the other side of the snap.

17. Trim the zipper so that it's not overhanging the edge.

18. Sew the two pocket layers to the exterior fabric across the bottom.

19. Sew around all of the layers.

20. Trim the edges with fabric scissors.

21. Turn the clutch almost completely inside out and sew the opening closed.

22. Turn the clutch all the way inside out and press the corners into place.

23. Attach your charm or keychain to the zipper.

24. Carry your new clutch wherever you need it!

Chapter 4
Projects and Ideas With Clothing

Projects and Ideas With Clothing The Cricut machines make it incredibly easy to customize clothing. Heat transfer vinyl can attach to any fabric and will last ages. All that you need for projects like these are the vinyl and a blank clothing item. You can find these just about anywhere, or you can get really crafty and sew your own. You can mix and match the designs and clothing you see here and, of course, come up with your own! The Cricut EasyPress will be your best friend for these projects since it heats up quickly and more evenly than regular iron.

There are almost as many types of heat transfer vinyl as regular vinyl. The Cricut brand alone has mosaic, glitter, glitter mesh, everyday, everyday mesh, holographic, holographic sparkle, lite, dark, foil, patterned, SportFlex, flocked, printable lite, and printable dark iron-on materials. You can choose whichever one matches the look you're going for. The SportFlex is designed to be thin and flexible and works well on fabrics like polyester and nylon. If you decide to use a mesh iron-on, keep your designs a little bit bigger.

Intricate designs won't work well on it.

Be sure to follow the specific instructions for the heat transfer vinyl you're using, as they can vary. Typically, you'll need to wash your clothing item before you use the vinyl. The chemicals that stores use to make the clothes more vibrant while on display will conflict with the heat transfer vinyl.

Prewashing also makes sure the clothing item shrinks if it's going to, so it won't interfere with your design in the future.

Project 23: Easy Lacey Dress

Easy Lacey Dress Lace dresses are adorable, but they can be hard to get ahold of and difficult to make. Fake it without anyone knowing better using your Cricut! The iron-on vinyl will look just like lace, and it will stand up to your child's activities much better than the real thing. Don't limit yourself to children's clothes; add some vinyl lace to your own as well! White vinyl will look like traditional lace the most, you can do this in any color that coordinates with the dress that you have. Use a Cricut EasyPress or iron to attach the vinyl to the fabric. You can use the Cricut Explore One, Cricut Explore Air 2, or Cricut Maker for this project.

Supplies Needed

- Dress of your choice
- White heat transfer vinyl
- Cricut EasyPress or iron
- Cutting mat
- Weeding tool or pick

Instructions

1. Open Cricut Design Space and create a new project.

2. Select the "Image" button in the lower left-hand corner and search

"vintage lace border."

3. Choose your favorite lace border and click "Insert."

4. Place your vinyl on the cutting mat.

5. Send the design to your Cricut.

6. Use a weeding tool or pick to remove the excess vinyl from the design.

7. Place the design along the hem of the dress with the plastic side up. Add lace wherever you like, such as along the collar or sleeves.

8. Carefully iron on the design.

9. After cooling, peel away the plastic by rolling it.

10. Dress your child up in her adorable lacey dress!

Project 24: Dinosaur T-Shirt

Dinosaur T-Shirt Everyone loves dinosaurs, and kids can't have enough t-shirts. Use iron-on vinyl to create the perfect shirt for your fossil-loving child! The small designs on the sleeves add a little extra, bringing it up a level from your standard graphic t-shirt. Just as with the rest of these projects, you can use the same idea with different designs. Customize a shirt for any of your child's interests. The Cricut EasyPress or iron will help you attach the vinyl designs to the t-shirt. You can use the Cricut Explore One, Cricut Explore Air 2, or Cricut Maker for this project.

Supplies Needed

- T-shirt of your choice

- Green heat transfer vinyl

- Cricut EasyPress or iron

- Cutting mat

- Weeding tool or pick

Instructions

1. Open Cricut Design Space.

2. Select the "Image" button in the lower left-hand corner and search

"dinosaur."

3. Choose your favorite dinosaur and click "Insert."

4. Select "Image" again and search for "fossils."

5. Choose your favorite fossil and click "Insert."

6. Copy the fossil once so that you have two of them.

7. Place your vinyl on the cutting mat.

8. Send the design to your Cricut.

9. Use a weeding tool or pick to remove the excess vinyl from the design.

10. Place the dinosaur in the center of the t-shirt, and a

fossil on each sleeve, with the plastic side up.

11. Carefully iron on the design.

12. After cooling, peel away the plastic by rolling it.

Project 25: Flower Garden Tote Bag

Flower Garden Tote Bag You can never have too many tote bags, whether you use them as reusable shopping bags, giant purses, or anything else. Create this cute flower garden bag to carry wherever you need to, and keep nature right by your side all day! Choose your favorite flowers, and the more variety you have, the more interesting the bag will be to look at. Canvas bags are a nice neutral base that will last you years, but you can use this idea with a different type of tote as well. The white vinyl gives a silhouette effect, but you can use a different color or even make each flower its own color. You'll need a Cricut EasyPress or iron for the heat transfer vinyl. You can use the Cricut Explore One, Cricut Explore Air 2, or Cricut Maker for this project.

Supplies Needed

- Canvas tote bag

- White heat transfer vinyl

- Cricut EasyPress or iron

- Cutting mat

- Weeding tool or pick

Instructions

1. Open Cricut Design Space and create a new project.

2. Select the "Image" button in the lower left-hand corner and search

"flowers."

3. Choose your favorite flower and click "Insert."

4. Continue with a variety of flowers, lining them up together to form a straight edge at the bottom.

5. Place your vinyl on the cutting mat.

6. Send the design to your Cricut.

7. Use a weeding tool or pick to remove the excess vinyl from the design.

8. Place the design along the bottom of the tote bag with the plastic

side up.

9. Carefully iron on the design.

10. After cooling, peel away the plastic by rolling it.

11. Carry around your new garden tote bag!

Chapter 5
Projects and Ideas With Glass

Projects and Ideas With Glass Vinyl cut with your Cricut machine can help you create beautiful glass projects. There are several different ways you can use it, as well. Any glass object can be a blank for these projects. You might already have some things in your kitchen that you'd like to decorate. These make wonderful gifts, too —no one will believe that you made them yourself and that they're not expensive gifts.

Glass etching cream is an interesting product that lets you easily create etched glass projects. There are several different brands that you can find at craft stores or online. You may be able to find them at hardware stores as well.

Read the instructions carefully and follow them exactly, to get your desired results and to be safe. It is actually an acid that eats away at the glass to create the etched effect. This may vary between brands, but often, stirring the cream around during its setting time will make the etching more pronounced. This will be a permanent effect on the glass.

Besides etching, you can also create beautiful glass projects using vinyl.

Outdoor vinyl, which is permanent, is the best choice if you want the design to stay put through use and washing. Removable vinyl will be temporary, and you can peel it off; it won't survive being washed. Window-cling vinyl sticks to glass via static, so they are quite temporary but can easily be changed out and reused.

Project 26: Etched Monogrammed Glass

Etched Monogrammed Glass Glasses are one of the most-used things in your kitchen, and it's impossible to have too many of them. It's actually quite easy to customize them with etching, and it will look as if a professional did it. Simply use glass etching cream that you can find at any craft store! Be sure to read the instructions and warning labels carefully before you begin. The vinyl will act as a stencil, protecting the parts of the glass that you don't want to etch. Be sure to take your time to get the vinyl smooth against the glass, especially where there are small bits. You don't want any of the cream to get under the edge of the vinyl. You can use the Cricut Explore One, Cricut Explore Air 2, or Cricut Maker for this project.

Supplies Needed

- A glass of your choice – make sure that the spot you want to monogram is smooth

- Vinyl

- Cutting mat

- Weeding tool or pick

- Glass etching cream

Instructions

1. Open Cricut Design Space and create a new project.

2. Select the "Image" button in the Design Panel and search for

"monogram."

3. Choose your favorite monogram and click "Insert."

4. Place your vinyl on the cutting mat.

5. Send the design to your Cricut.

6. Use a weeding tool or pick to remove the monogram, leaving the vinyl around it.

7. Remove the vinyl from the mat.

8. Carefully apply the vinyl around your glass, making it as smooth

as possible, particularly around the monogram.

9. If you have any letters with holes in your monogram, carefully reposition those cutouts in their proper place.

10. Following the instructions on the etching cream, apply it to your monogram.

11. Remove the cream and then the vinyl.

12. Give your glass a good wash.

Project 27: Live, Love, Laugh Glass Block

Glass blocks are an inexpensive yet surprisingly versatile craft material. You can find them at both craft and hardware stores. They typically have a hole with a lid so that you can fill the blocks with the items of your choice.

This project uses tiny fairy lights for a glowing quote block, but you can fill it however you'd like. The frost spray paint adds a bit of elegance to the glass and diffuses the light for a softer glow, hiding the string of the fairy lights.

Holographic vinyl will add to the magical look, but you can use whatever colors you'd like. This features a classic quote that's great to have around your house, but you can change it. You can use the Cricut Explore One, Cricut Explore Air 2, or Cricut Maker for this project.

Supplies Needed

- Glass block

- Frost spray paint

- Clear enamel spray

- Holographic vinyl

- Vinyl transfer tape

- Cutting mat

- Weeding tool or pick

- Fairy lights

Instructions

1. Spray the entire glass block with frost spray paint, and let it dry.

2. Spray the glass block with a coat of clear enamel spray, and let it dry.

3. Open Cricut Design Space and create a new project.

4. Select the "Text" button in the Design Panel.

5. Type "Live Love Laugh" in the text box.

6. Use the dropdown box to select your favorite font.

7. Arrange the words to sit on top of each other.

8. Place your vinyl on the cutting mat.

9. Send the design to your Cricut.

10. Use a weeding tool or pick to remove the excess vinyl from the design.

11. Apply transfer tape to the design.

12. Remove the paper backing and apply the words to the glass block.

13. Smooth down the design and carefully remove the transfer tape.

14. Place fairy lights in the opening of the block, leaving the battery pack on the outside.

Project 28: Unicorn Wine Glass

Who doesn't love unicorns? Who doesn't love wine? Bring them together with these glittery wine glasses! The outdoor vinyl will hold up to use and washing, and the Mod Podge will keep the glitter in place for years to come. Customize it even more with your own quote. You could use a different magical creature as well— mermaids go great with glitter too! Customize this to suit your tastes or to create gifts for your friends and family. Consider using these for a party and letting the guests take them home as favors! You can use the Cricut Explore One, Cricut Explore Air 2, or Cricut Maker for this project.

Supplies Needed

- Stemless wine glasses

- Outdoor vinyl in the color of your choice

- Vinyl transfer tape

- Cutting mat

- Weeding tool or pick

- Extra fine glitter in the color of your choice Mod Podge

Instructions

1. Open Cricut Design Space and create a new project.

2. Select the "Text" button in the Design Panel.

3. Type "It's not drinking alone if my unicorn is here."

4. Using the dropdown box, select your favorite font.

5. Adjust the positioning of the letters, rotating some to give a whimsical look.

6. Select the "Image" button on the Design Panel and search for

"unicorn."

7. Select your favorite unicorn and click "Insert," then arrange your design how you want it on the glass.

8. Place your vinyl on the cutting mat, making sure it is smooth and making full contact.

9. Send the design to your Cricut.

10. Use a weeding tool or pick to remove the excess vinyl from the design. Use the Cricut BrightPad to help if you have one.

11. Apply transfer tape to the design, pressing firmly and making sure there are no bubbles.

12. Remove the paper backing and apply the words to the glass where you'd like them. Leave at least a couple of inches at the bottom for the glitter.

13. Smooth down the design and carefully remove the transfer tape.

14. Coat the bottom of the glass in Mod Podge, wherever you would like glitter to be. Give the area a wavy edge.

15. Sprinkle glitter over the Mod Podge, working quickly before it dries.

16. Add another layer of Mod Podge and glitter, and set it aside to dry.

17. Cover the glitter in a thick coat of Mod Podge.

18. Allow the glass to cure for at least 48 hours.

500 More Ideas to Spark Your Imagination

The possibilities with your Cricut are nearly infinite. The projects in previous chapters cover a wide array of techniques, methods, and materials, but they're only a fraction of what the Cricut machines are capable of. We could fill an entire library with project instructions! Instead of doing that, look through this list of words and phrases, and see what they spark in your mind. You could use them as project titles and create something that fits it, or it could be the inspiration that lets you come up with something completely different.

They could even act as components for a larger project.

Here are 500 more ideas to inspire you. Take these phrases and create a project with them!

1. Pet food and water bowls

2. Kitchen dry goods storage

3. Pool toys

4. Holiday mug

5. Etched casserole dish

6. Custom cooking utensils

7. Quote sweatshirt

8. Patterned tiles

9. Giant wall art

10. Paper banners

11. Paper sculptures

12. Vinyl Christmas tree

13. Treat bags

14. Party favors

15. Cake decorations

16. Gift boxes

17. Custom kid's ornaments

18. Party place settings

19. Origami

20. Handmade cards

21. Bookmarks

22. Refrigerator magnets

23. Chalkboards

24. Dry erase labels

25. Music picture frame

26. Desk organizer

27. Easter baskets

28. Personalized tools

29. Etched Mason jars

30. Wine or champagne glass markers

31. Canvas art

32. Decorative plates

33. Ice cream bowls

34. Party games

35. Halloween masks

36. Wine bottle lamps

37. Valentines

38. Candy holders

39. Wooden signs

40. Beach bag

41. Drink holders

42. Mug warmers

43. Pencil pouch

44. Calligraphy wall art

45. Customized lap desk

46. Breakfast-in-bed tray

47. Coffee bar sign

48. Cookie jar

49. Crafting stamps

50. Planner stickers

51. Custom calendar

52. Journal pages

53. Welcome mat

54. Wine gift bag

55. Silhouette art

56. Art storage

57. Labeled laundry baskets

58. Customized travel mugs

59. State silhouette signs

60. Forest themed nursery décor

61. Candle holders

62. Custom shot glasses

63. Wedding favors

64. Book tote bag

65. Patterned wood letters

66. Quilled art

67. Team t-shirts

68. Teacher appreciation mug gifts

69. Photo booth props

70. Personalized bottle cap catcher

71. Wine cork box

72. Paper succulents

73. Patterned scarf

74. Designed umbrella

75. Mandala hoodie

76. 3D stars

77. Doll clothing

78. Custom jigsaw puzzle

79. Glitter tumblers

80. Labeled pantry bins

81. Kitchen conversions chart

82. Family center

83. Paper straw party decorations

84. Headbands

85. Personalized tea towels

86. Stained glass wind chime

87. Ring dish

88. Monogrammed throw pillow

89. Giant bows

90. Kitchen mixer decals

91. Custom onesies

92. Car window decals

93. Hanging planter

94. Bumper stickers

95. Paper flower wreath

96. Nursery mobile

97. Food pun dish towels

98. Customized beach towel

99. Drink cooler

100. Pendant necklace

101. Leather tassel earrings

102. Finger puppets

103. 3D puzzles

104. Charity shirts

105. Glass cutting board

106. Wooden family name sign

107. Notebook covers

108. Flip flops

109. Decorative hand mirror

110. Makeup storage

111. Pop up paper animals

112. Felt flowers

113. Quilts

114. Vinyl banners

115. Custom pot holders

116. Thank you cards

117. Leather purse

118. Dry erase weekly menu

119. Cookies for Santa plate and mug

120. Family tree wall art

121. Photo magnets

122. Window clings

123. Felt headband

124. Tupperware for food gifts

125. Sleep mask

126. Microwaveable rice pack

127. Leather cuff bracelet

128. Custom ballcaps

129. Decorated dog bandanas

130. Tooth fairy bags

131. Coloring books

132. Pop up cards

133. Polka dot vase

134. Winter shadowbox

135. Drink koozies

136. Custom drawer pulls

137. Photo board

138. Planner pages

139. Balsa wood jewelry

140. Etched pet tags

141. Water measurement bottle

142. Etched measuring glass

143. Countdown sign

144. Workout tank top

145. Large wall decals

146. Embossed cards

147. Chipboard letters

148. Striped coffee mug

149. Tea bag holder

150. Decorative tea light holders

151. Foam stamps

152. Llama mask

153. Price tags

154. Paper pinwheels

155. Address labels

156. Faux leather initial pendant

157. Felt flower hair clip

158. Earring cards

159. Treat packaging

160. Paper lanterns

161. Baby milestone blanket

162. Cupcake gift box

163. Custom mittens

164. Silhouette candle jar

165. Wood name keychain

166. Faux leather luggage tag

167. Paper cut art

168. School year backpack

169. Hangry apron

170. Father's Day cake topper

171. Galaxy coasters

172. Wedding table numbers

173. Passport holder

174. Nightlight cover

175. Foodie lunch box

176. Paper fans

177. Geometric canvas art

178. Pencil roll

179. Growth chart

180. Classroom bulletin board

181. Patterned phone case

182. Seasonal placemats

183. Child's handprint art

184. Dog/cat collar decorations

185. Memory match game

186. Dog/cat bed

187. Napkin rings

188. Christmas stockings

189. Party menus

190. Leather flower keychain

191. Sticker sheets

192. Custom craft apron

193. Pegboard organization

194. Chore chart

195. Shabby chic sign

196. Shoe bins

197. Stamped leather bracelet

198. Dreamcatcher canvas

199. Quote phone case

200. Stuffed felt toys

201. Take out favor boxes

202. Shaped confetti

203. Halloween monster wreath

204. Saint Patrick's Day four-leafed clovers

205. Monogrammed Christmas bulbs

206. Lesson plan binder

207. Recipe cards

208. Giant Scrabble tiles

209. Scrapbook layouts

210. Dress-up trunk

211. History diorama

212. Pinewood derby car

213. Marshmallow slingshot

214. Themed cupcake liners

215. Princess party favors

216. Autumn leaf décor

217. Metal etchings

218. Paper quill pens

219. Decorative crystals

220. Party invitations

221. Cookie boxes

222. Doll clothes

223. Buffet dish labels

224. Advanced paper airplanes

225. Ship in a bottle

226. Hand bound sketchbook

227. Name tags

228. Infinity scarf

229. Magnetic bookmark

230. Chore chart

231. Meal planning notebook

232. Bingo boards

233. School folders

234. Science fair board

235. Lamp shades

236. Tissue paper tiki torches

237. Jack O' Lantern templates

238. Craft kit gifts

239. Piñata

240. Multi pocket pencil case

241. Family photo album

242. Paper cranes

243. Easter egg tree

244. Play swords

245. Cardboard fort

246. Scrapbook pages

247. Leather pyramid purse

248. Caterpillar pencil pouch

249. Workbooks

250. Classroom activities

251. Birthday crown

252. Faux fur pocketbook

253. Paper dolls

254. Costume glasses

255. Superhero cape

256. Felted animals

257. Leather pet collar

258. Swatch card

259. Artist trading cards

260. Educational poster

261. Clock face

262. Inspiration board

263. Badges/buttons

264. Tissue paper ghosts

265. Wooden utensils

266. Pen wraps

267. Phone charger covers

268. Assignment book

269. Desktop calendar

270. Tablet case

271. Outdoor banner

272. Yard sale sign

273. Wooden marketplace sign

274. Reading chart

275. Bird whistle

276. Paper lei

277. Map poster

278. Scratch off cards

279. Faux stained glass window clings

280. Comic book pages

281. Book covers

282. Etched wood picture frame

283. Aged chalkboard sign

284. Chipboard bookends

285. Etched ceramic tea set

286. Dry erase wall

287. Drawer dividers

288. Toy car race track

289. Party drink dispensers

290. Shaped wood cutting board

291. State string art

292. Road trip planner

293. Potato stamps

294. Giant paper butterflies

295. Award medals

296. Marble tracks

297. Suede makeup bag

298. Faux leather passport cover

299. Monitor border

300. Snake necklace

301. Play wizard wands

302. Phone wrap sticker

303. Bedside organizer

304. Marble coasters

305. Mosaic vase

306. Bejeweled heart keychain

307. Woven leather ring

308. Envelope clutch

309. Fuzzy winter socks

310. Bubble cups

311. Lace table runner

312. Hamster/guinea pig/mouse toys

313. Shaped toss pillows

314. Confetti scrunchies

315. Book club mugs

316. Dream journal

317. File folder labels

318. Custom salt cellar

319. Flowery play tea set

320. Bug net

321. Document pouch

322. First aid kit

323. Embroidered handkerchief

324. Pool rules sign

325. Swirled ear cuff

326. Fish tank decorations

327. Scavenger hunt

328. Shot glass party favors

329. Keepsake glass box

330. Lace gloves

331. Display cabinet

332. Food labels

333. Garden markers

334. Bible case

335. Lettering practice sheet

336. Wall mural stencils

337. Paper doilies

338. Graffiti banner

339. Freezer organizers

340. Pet food bin

341. Snowflake garland

342. Rosebud headband

343. Custom hair clips

344. Christmas tree topper

345. Felt shamrocks

346. Bird house

347. Weather board

348. Braided rug

349. Ragdoll

350. Collage photo frame

351. Chocolate wrappers

352. Fanny pack

353. Embroidered calendar

354. Cosplay armor

355. Pin display

356. Baby blanket

357. Coffee tin

358. Award certificate

359. Paper party straws

360. Fill-in-the-blank games

361. Marker stand

362. Flower fairy lights

363. Antiqued cake stand

364. Drawstring backpack

365. Art portfolio

366. Weekly menu board

367. Sports team water bottles

368. Raffle tickets

369. Tea box

370. Wallpaper decal

371. Custom postage stamps

372. Shaped mousepad

373. Pizza slice holders

374. Invoices

375. Glitter containers

376. Dollhouse furniture

377. Custom paint palette

378. Cloth patches

379. Acrylic stamp

380. Resin rings

381. Crystal ball

382. Fortune cookie fortunes

383. Address book

384. Marathon runner numbers

385. Class election posters

386. Succulent centerpieces

387. Window herb garden

388. Fish mask

389. Pool diving toys

390. Soap dish

391. Etched serving bowl

392. Dog leash charms

393. Wooden monogram decoration

394. Reminder magnets

395. Information pamphlets

396. Pen pal envelopes

397. Custom baseball cards

398. Bookshelf labels

399. Mystery box

400. Sequined necklace

401. Game board

402. Dry erase plant pots

403. Monogrammed cigar box

404. Cat/dog toy box

405. Game cartridge storage

406. Progress poster

407. Motivational gym bag

408. Medication chart

409. Allergen bracelet

410. Baby book

411. Glasses holder necklace

412. Beaded edge blanket

413. Temperature record scarf

414. Personalized watch band

415. Health log

416. Lesson plans

417. Paper grass

418. Etched border mirror

419. DVD/game disc storage

420. Connect the dot games

421. Star chart

422. Witch's cauldron mug

423. Unicorn acrylic necklace

424. Plastic bugs

425. Refrigerator poetry magnets

426. Flowered flip flops

427. Non-slip coasters

428. Celestial hair pins

429. Birthstone brooch

430. Custom buttons

431. Tin punch signs

432. Washi tape holder

433. Dinosaur toothbrush holder 434. Handprint vase

435. Sewing patterns

436. Mail organizer

437. Felt play sets

438. Etched wedding champagne flutes

439. Alien costume

440. Spray painted sign

441. Tie-dye shirt with cutout design

442. Spooky eye Halloween window clings

443. Iced tea pitcher

444. Lemonade stand sign

445. Floating foam bath toys

446. Glass soap/lotion dispensers

447. Leather coin purse

448. Health and safety sign

449. Patterned pajama pants

450. Hand sewn moccasins

451. Ceiling light pull chain

452. Paper dragon

453. Bumblebee costume wings

454. Drink recipe tumbler

455. Burlap sack

456. Woven storage basket

457. Glitter star confetti

458. Balsa wood cake topper

459. Striped popcorn bucket

460. Framed calligraphy quotes

461. Purse organizer with pockets

462. Manicure templates

463. Recipe printed cookie tin

464. Decorated fruit bowl

465. Felt costume hats

466. Building brick toy storage

467. Play kitchen set

468. Mug cake recipe printed mug

469. Etched mason jar drinking glasses

470. Birthday signs

471. Dog shirts

472. Play ninja stars

473. Holographic pinwheels

474. Glitter bumper sticker

475. Key tags

476. Lottery games

477. Paper quilling art

478. Cleaning supply storage

479. Embossed leather band

480. Velvety slippers

481. Dog booties

482. Baby month onesies

483. Matching shampoo/conditioner/body wash containers 484. Potpourri sachets

485. Closet deodorizers

486. Thanksgiving cornucopia decorations

487. Pop culture based props

488. Labels for homemade cosmetics

489. Recycled paper garlands

490. Family values wood sign

491. Custom tablecloth

492. Embossed holiday cards

493. Cardboard cutouts

494. Novelty sunglasses

495. Etched inkwell

496. Tiled wall clock

497. Desk catch-all

498. Mug sweater

499. 3D chipboard puzzles

500. Origami vase

Chapter 6: FAQ

1. Where can I use Cricut Design Space?

You can use Cricut Design Space through your web browser on PC or Mac after downloading the plugin. You can also download the app on your tablet or smartphone on iOS or Android.

2. How does my machine connect to Design Space?

Explore Air 2 has built-in Bluetooth, so it can connect to any device that has that capability. The Explore One has to be connected directly to your computer, or you can purchase a Cricut Wireless Bluetooth Adapter.

3. What is Cricut Access?

This is Cricut's subscription service to their library of images and fonts in Cricut Design Space. It gives access to more than 30,000 images, 370 fonts, and premium project ideas, as well as 10% off all purchases on the Cricut website. There are different types of plans available, ranging from $4.99 to $9.99 per month.

4. How do I install Design Space?

Open your web browser and enter design.cricut.com into the address bar. Sign in with your Cricut ID, or create one if you haven't yet. After signing in, select New Project. Design Space will give you a prompt to download and install the plugin. Click Download and wait for it to finish. Once it does, click the file to install the plugin. You might get a box asking for permission; if so, allow it. Follow the prompts through the installer. You're now ready to use Design Space!

5. Why am I getting error messages about the Design Space plugin?

If you're getting error messages or having difficulty using Design Space, you may need to reinstall the plugin. Expand your computer's system tray in the lower right-hand side of the screen and locate the Cricut icon. Right-click on it and click Exit. Open your web browser and navigate to design.cricut.com and sign in with your Cricut ID.

Once prompted, download and install the plugin again.

6. Do I need a computer to use my Cricut machine?

No! If you have the Cricut Explore Air or the Cricut Maker, you can utilize the built-in Bluetooth to connect to your mobile device and download the Design Space app on it.

7. What's the difference between the Cricut Explore One and the Cricut Explore Air 2?

The Cricut Explore One has a single tool carriage, so if you do more than one action (cut and write or cut and score), it will need to do it in two steps, and you'll need to switch out the tools between them. The Cricut Explore Air 2 has two tool carriages, so it can do both functions in one step with no need to switch tools. Explore Air 2 also has built-in Bluetooth connectivity.

8. Do I use the same Cricut Design Space for the Cricut Maker?

Yes! The only difference is that you'll have the option to

adjust the material settings in the Design Space since the Maker does not have the dial on the machine itself.

9. How does the Cricut Maker know which blade is in the carriage?

The machine scans the blade before it cuts a project.

10. What is the thickness of a material that the Cricut Maker can cut?

3/32" of an inch or 2.4mm when using the rotary blade or the knife blade.

11. How do I get a good transfer using the Cricut EasyPress?

Use the EasyPress on a firm and even surface. Check the iron-on material and the base material for the recommended settings and use those. Be sure to apply heat to both the front and back of the project for the recommended amount of time.

12. How much pressure does the Cricut EasyPress

need?

Check the recommendations for the material you're using. Some will call for "firm" pressure, meaning you should use two hands and about 15–20 lbs of body weight. Others need "gentle" pressure, meaning you should use one hand with about 5–10 lbs of body weight. Use your EasyPress on a waist-high table for the easiest way to apply pressure.

13. Do I move the Cricut EasyPress around like an iron?

Keep the EasyPress in one spot for the recommended amount of time.

Moving it might smear or warp the design.

14. Why should I use the Cricut EasyPress?

It heats more evenly and more quickly than iron and is easy to use. It will give you more professional-looking iron-ons and takes 60 seconds or less.

15. How do I protect surfaces while using the Cricut

EasyPress?

Cricut recommends using the Cricut EasyPress mat, which comes in three different sizes. However, you can also use a cotton bath towel with an even texture folded to about 3 inches thick. Do not use an ironing board, as the surface isn't even enough, and it's too unsteady to apply appropriate pressure. Silicone baking mats and aluminum foil don't provide enough insulation and can get dangerously hot.

16. My material is tearing! Why?

The most common reason is that your mat isn't sticky enough. It could have lost its stickiness, or you aren't using the right mat for the material. It could also be that the blade needs to be replaced or sharpened, or you're using the wrong type of blade. Materials can also tear if the machine is on the wrong setting.

17. Why won't my transfer tape work?

More often than not, it's not working when you try to use standard transfer tape with glitter vinyl. It requires the Cricut Strong Grip transfer tape. It's too strong to use with regular vinyl, though, so keep using the regular transfer tape for that.

18. What type of mat should I use?

Each mat has a specific use. Here's each one and some suggestions of what material to use with them.

Blue: Light Grip Mat – Thinner paper, vellum, construction paper, sticky notes, light vinyl, and wrapping paper Green: Standard Grip Mat – Cardstock, thicker paper, washi paper, vinyl, and bonded fabric

Purple: Strong Grip Mat – Thick cardstock, magnet sheets, chipboard, poster board, fabric with stiffener, aluminum foil, foam, leather, and suede

Pink: Fabric Grip Mat – Fabric, bonded fabric, and crepe paper

19. How do I wash my mats?

Place the mat in the sink, supported by a firm flat

surface. Running lukewarm water over it, use a hard-bristled brush to scrub it gently in circles until the mat is clean. Pat dry with a paper towel, and let it air dry for the stickiness to return.

20. Why won't my blade cut all the way through the material?

Make sure that the blade is completely in the carriage, and make sure there's no debris around it. Check that your settings are for the correct material. If you're still having trouble, slowly increase the pressure and do test cuts until it gets all the way through.

21. Can I upload my own images to the Cricut Design Space?

Yes! It's easy to upload your own image and create a design with it.

On the left side of Design Space, there is an option for "Upload Images."

22. What is infusible ink?

Infusible ink is a new system from Cricut that infuses ink directly into compatible Cricut blanks. There are infusible ink transfer sheets and infusible ink Pens and Markers. They are applied using heat, such as with the Cricut EasyPress.

23. Which machines can I use with Cricut Design Space?

Cricut Maker, Cricut Explore, Cricut Explore Air, Cricut Explore Air 2, and Cricut Explore One all work with Cricut Design Space.

24. Does Cricut Design Space require an internet connection?

Yes.

25. What weight is Cricut Cardstock?

80 lb

26. What are the care instructions for Cricut Iron-on

material?

Wash and dry the item inside out on the delicate style. If you notice areas of the iron-on material coming off after being washed, iron it again, following the full application instructions.

27. What's a quick reference list of materials I can cut?

For the Explore machines: all paper, all cardstock, vinyl, bonded fabrics, corrugated paper, sticker paper, and parchment paper. For the Maker machine: all of the above, plus fabric and textiles and thin wood.

28. Do I have to use Cricut brand materials?

No! You can use any brand of materials that you want. Thickness and quality are the only things that matter.

29. What pens can I use in my Cricut machine?

The Cricut brand pens will, of course, fit into your machine. However, some others will fit in the pen holder as well. Some users have found ways to adapt other pens, but the pens and markers in the following list don't require any adjustments.

Wal-Mart Leisure Arts Markers

Target Dual Tip Markers

Pilot Precise V5 pens

Thin Crayola markers

Dollar Tree Jot markers

Bic Round Stic pen

30. What is the Cricut Adaptive Tool System?

This is a new feature in the Cricut Maker. It adjusts the direction and pressure of the blades throughout the cutting process. It allows for much more precise cuts and much higher cutting pressure.

31. What is the difference between the different blades?

Fine Point Blade – This is the blade that comes in the box with all of the machines. It's made of German Carbide. It's designed to cut medium-weight materials, including printer paper, vinyl, cardstock, washi tape, parchment paper, vellum, canvas, light chipboard, and very thin faux leather.

Deep Point Blade – This blade is made for thicker materials and has a steeper angle—60 degrees—instead of the Fine Point's 45 degrees. It can cut craft foam, aluminum foil, genuine leather, metallic leather, magnetic sheet, and corrugated paper.

Bonded Fabric Blade – This is for use exclusively on bonded fabric. A bonded fabric has a backing, such as Heat and Bond, adhered to it. Without the backing, the fabric will tear and stretch, and it may damage your mat. It can cut the bonded forms of oilcloth, silk, polyester, denim, felt, burlap, and cotton.

Rotary Blade – This blade is only for the Cricut Maker and is included in the box. It utilizes the Adaptive Tool System.

It can cut fabric without it being bonded. The materials you cut with this blade should be at least ¾ of an inch or 19mm thick, so as not to damage the blade. It can cut all fabric, including bamboo fabric, bengaline, canvas, cashmere, chiffon, corduroy, cotton, denim, felt, fleece, gauze, silk, lycra, microfiber, and nylon.

Knife Blade – This is the other blade that comes in the box with the Cricut Maker. It can cut very thick materials. It gets through the same materials as the other blades, as well as tooling leather, balsa wood, basswood, heavy chipboard, and matboard.

32. What is the scoring wheel?

A scoring wheel is a tool for the Cricut Maker, as it uses the Adaptive Tool System. It creates fold lines in thicker materials. The Scoring Stylus also makes fold lines, but the Scoring Wheel is more powerful and can score thicker materials.

33. How small can the rotary blade cut?

Cricut recommends keeping designs above ¾". Any

smaller than that, the blade might gouge into your mat as it turns, damaging the mat and dulling the blade.

34. Where do I buy Cricut Blades?

You can buy blades where Cricut brand products are sold, including craft stores, superstores, Cricut's website, and other online stores.

35. What is the Fast Mode?

This is a feature on the Cricut Explore Air 2 and Cricut Maker. It allows you to cut and write twice as fast when the machine is set to vinyl, iron-on, or cardstock.

36. What is the Custom material setting for?

If you're cutting something besides paper, vinyl, iron-on, cardstock, fabric, or poster board on the Cricut Explore or Cricut Maker, you can choose Custom. This will open the material menu in Cricut Design Space. Select "Browse All Materials" and select the correct one. If you don't see your material listed, you can choose something close or create your own. If you create a custom material, you'll adjust the cut pressure, set if it uses multi-cut, and select the blade type. For help, you can look at the settings for something close to the material you're using. If you have enough of the material, do several tests with different settings to see what works best.

37. How do I calibrate my Cricut for Print then Cut?

In Design Space, select the menu (three lines) in the upper right-hand corner. Select Calibration, Print, and Cut. Choose your printer and select Print. Your printer will create a calibration sheet. Take this sheet and place it on your Cricut mat in the top left-hand corner. Click Continue in Design Space. Select your machine from the dropdown menu, then the material setting. Load the mat and press the Go button.

The machine will proceed to scan the calibration sheet and use the markings to calibrate itself. When it's done, it will cut out the small square near the center of the sheet. Without unloading the mat, check that the cut touches the printed line all the way around the shape. If it does, click Yes in Design Space. Next, the machine will make the calibration cuts at the top and sides of the page. Without unloading the mat, check the position of the cuts relative to the printed lines. Some will be touching, and others will not. In Design Space, select the Top and Right dropdowns to enter the line number or letter where the cuts are closest to the center of the line. Click Continue. Finally, the machine will cut around the large rectangle. Unload the mat and remove the calibration sheet. Answer the last question in Design Space. If the calibration looks okay to you, click Yes. If it doesn't, click No, and you will be walked through the calibration process again in an attempt to fix it. After reaching the final screen, click Save and Close. Your machine is now calibrated for Print then Cut.

38. Why is my Print then Cut image printing too large?

Your text and image scaling on your computer may be set above 100%, and this will make your printed images larger. You'll need to change this setting back to 100%. Right-click anywhere on your computer's desktop and click Display Settings. Below the Customize Your Display box, there is a slider or dropdown box labeled "Change the size of text, apps, and other items." Change it to 100%. Click Apply, then restart your computer.

39. Why does Design Space say my Cricut machine is already in use when it's not?

To resolve this, make sure that you've completed the New Machine Setup for your Cricut. Try Design Space in another browser. The two that work best are Google Chrome and Mozilla Firefox; if it doesn't work in one of those, try the other. If that doesn't clear the error, try a different USB port and USB cable. Disconnect the machine from the computer and turn it off. While it's off, restart your computer. After your computer restarts, reconnect the machine and turn it on. Wait a few moments, then try Design Space again. If you're still having the same problem, contact Cricut Member Care.

40. Why doesn't my cut match the preview in Design Space?

Test another image and see if the same thing happens. If it's only happening with the one project, create a new project and start over or try a different image. If it happens with a second project, and your machine is connected with Bluetooth, disconnect that and plug it in with a USB cable. Larger projects may sometimes have difficulty communicating the cuts over Bluetooth. If you can't connect with USB

or the problem is still occurring, check that your computer matches or exceeds the system requirements for running Design Space. If it doesn't, try the project on a different computer or mobile device that does. If your computer does meet the requirements, open Design Space in a different browser and try again. If the problem continues, try a different USB cable. Finally, if the issue still hasn't resolved, contact Cricut Member Care.

41. What do I do if I need to install USB drivers for my Cricut machine?

Typically, the Cricut drivers are automatically installed when you connect it with a USB cable. If Design Space doesn't see your machine, you can try this to troubleshoot the driver installation. First, open Device

Manager on your computer. You'll need to have administrator rights. For Windows 7, click Start, right-click on Computer, and select Manage. For Windows 8 and up, right-click on the Start icon and click Computer Management. Within Computer Management, click Device Manager on the left-hand side. Find your Cricut machine on the list—it should be listed under Ports, but it might be under Other Devices or Universal Serial Bus Controllers. Right-click on it and select Update Driver Software. In the box that pops up, select Browse My Computer. In the box on the next screen, type in

%APPDATA% and click Browse. Another box will pop up where you can search through folders. Find AppData and expand it. Click Roaming, then CricutDesignSpace, then Web, then Drivers, then CricutDrivers, and click OK. Click Next to install these drivers. Once it's finished, restart your computer. Once it's on, open Design Space again to see if it recognizes your machine.

42. Why does my Cricut Maker say the blade is not detected?

Make sure that the tool in Clamp B is the same one

Design Space recommends in the Load Tools step of the Project Preview screen. If you don't have that recommended tool, unload your mat and select Edit Tools on the Project Preview screen. Here, you can select a different tool. If the tool and the selection already match, carefully remove the tool from Clamp B and clean the reflective band on the housing. Reinstall it in the clamp and press the Go button. If that doesn't resolve the problem, remove the tool again, and clean the sensor inside the machine. Reinstall the tool and press Go again. If the Maker still doesn't detect the blade, try a simple test project using a basic shape with one of the other tools. If that works, there may be something wrong with the drive housing of the original tool. If the problem continues with other tools, or you don't have another tool to test, trying uninstalling and reinstalling Design Space and retry your project. If the issue persists, or if you've discovered it's an issue with the tool housing, contact Cricut Member Care.

43. Why is my Cricut machine making a grinding noise?

If it's the carriage car making a loud noise after you press the cut button, and it sounds like the carriage might be hitting the side of the machine, record a short video of it and send it to Cricut Member Care.

If the noise is coming from a brand-new machine the first time you use it, contact Cricut Member Care. Otherwise, make sure that you're using the original power cord that came with your machine. If the machine isn't getting the correct voltage, it may produce a grinding sound. If you are using the machine's power cord, adjust your pressure settings. If it's too high, it might produce an unusual sound. Decrease it in increments of 2–4, and do some test cuts. If it's still making the issue even after decreasing the cutting pressure, contact Cricut Member Care.

44. What if my Cricut is making a different loud noise?

Make sure that you don't have Fast Mode engaged for cutting or writing. If it's not on, take a short video of the problem to send to

Cricut Member Care.

45. Why is my mat going into the machine crooked?

Check the roller bar to see if it's loose, damaged, or uneven. If it is, take a photo or video of it to send to Cricut Member Care. If the roller bar seems fine, make sure that you're using the right mat size for the machine. Next, make sure the mat is correctly lined up with the guides and that the edge is underneath the roller bar when you prepare to load it. If it's still loading crookedly even when properly lined up with the guides, try applying gentle pressure to the mat to get it under the roller bar once it starts. If none of this works, contact Cricut Member Care.

46. Why isn't the Smart Set Dial changing the material in Design Space?

Make sure that the USB cable between the computer and the Cricut Explore is properly connected. If so, disconnect the Explorer from the computer and turn it off. Restart your computer. Once it's on, turn on the Explore, plug it into the computer, and try the cut again. If it still isn't changing the material, connect the USB cable to a different port on the computer. If it's still not working, try Design Space in multiple web browsers and see if the problem replicates. If it does, try an entirely different USB cable. Check for Firmware Updates for the Explore. If you don't have another USB cable, the Firmware Update doesn't help, or there are no Firmware Updates, contact Cricut Member Care.

47. What do I do if my Cricut Maker stopped partway through a cut?

If the Knife Blade stops cutting and the Go button is flashing, the Maker has encountered some sort of error. In Design Space, you'll get a notification that the blade is stuck. This might have been caused by the blade running into something like a knot or seam if too much dust or debris built up in the cut area or if the blade got into a gouge in the mat from a previous cut. To resume your project, do not unload the mat. This will lose your place in the project, and it will be impossible to get it lined up again. Check the cut area for dust or debris, and gently clean it. If there's dust on top of Clamp B, brush it off with a clean, dry paintbrush. Do not remove the blade. Once the debris is gone, press the Go button. The machine will take a moment to sense the Knife Blade again, and then it will resume cutting.

48. Why is my fabric getting caught under the rollers?

If the fabric extends past the adhesive area of the Fabric Grip mat, it will run into the rubber rollers on either side of the roller bar. The rubber rollers grip the fabric and pull it, making it crooked or getting it caught in the machine. Be sure to cut down any fabric so that it fits on your mat without going past the adhesive. If you have stuck the fabric and realize it's hanging past the adhesive, use a ruler and a sharp blade to trim it. Or, if it's the correct size but slightly askew, unstick it and reposition it.

49. Why would my Cricut Maker continuously turn off during cuts?

This can happen from a build-up of static electricity while cutting foil and metal sheets. Makers in dry areas are more susceptible to this.

Spritzing water in the air will dissipate the build-up. Be careful not to spray any water directly on the Maker. Using a humidifier or vaporizer in the area where you use your Maker can help avoid the static build-ups. If this doesn't seem to be what's causing the issue, contact Cricut Member Care.

50. What do I do about a failing or incomplete firmware update?

Be sure to use a computer to install the firmware update and that you're connected with a USB cable rather than Bluetooth. Verify that the computer meets the minimum system requirements; if it doesn't, you'll need to use another computer that does. If it does and you're still having problems, disconnect the Cricut from your computer and turn it off. Restart the computer. Once it's back on, open Design Space and try the firmware update again. If it still freezes up or doesn't complete, try the update using a different web browser. The next step is to try another USB cable. If that doesn't help, or you don't have another USB cable to try, contact Cricut Member Care.

51. What do I do if my Cricut machine is having power issues?

If your Cricut Maker, Cricut Explore One, or Cricut Explore Air 2 is having issues with power, these are the troubleshooting steps. If the machine doesn't have any power or only has it sometimes, make sure that the plug is completely plugged into the power port on the machine, the power adapter, and the wall outlet. The cutting mat can sometimes knock the power cable loose as it goes through the machine. You can avoid this by making sure the excess cord isn't bundled up behind the machine. If everything is securely plugged in, make sure that you're using the genuine Cricut power cable that came with your machine and that the green light on the adapter is lit up. If you're not using the Cricut power cable, you can buy one or contact Cricut Member Care. If you are, try using a different wall outlet. If it's still having problems, try another Cricut power cable. If the issues continue even after this, take a short video of the issue happening and forward it to Cricut Member Care.

52. What do I do if I'm having issues with the machine's door?

If the door won't open or won't stay open, take a short

video to forward on to Cricut Member Care. If the door won't close or won't stay closed, make sure there aren't any accessories loaded into the accessory clamp. If there aren't, take a photo or short video to forward to the Cricut Member Care team.

53. Why does my Cricut EasyPress 2 keep shutting off?

The EasyPress 2 has a safety feature that turns it off after 10 minutes without use. If there have been no activity or button presses, the machine will give you an alert and then turn itself off

Conclusion

Thank you for making it to the end of Cricut Project Ideas! Let's hope it was informative and able to provide you with a lot of inspiration and new ideas for your Cricut machine.

The next step is to experiment with your Cricut machine and all of the materials you can use with it. The projects in this book only cover a small portion of what the Cricut is capable of. Refer back to the first and second chapter for some more ideas of materials you can try and where you'll be able to find them.

Tweak the ideas in this book to fit you perfectly. Change up the materials, the blanks, what the design is, and whatever else your imagination can come up with. Create your own projects, as well. Following the ideas in this book will give you a good foundation for using your Cricut. Once you've become familiar with it in the different ways that you can use it, you can let your creativity flow and create whatever you want.

For more inspiration, you can check out more books that are similar to this one, or browse project ideas online. Cricut's website features a lot of project ideas, and the Cricut Design Space has some premade projects and templates that you can use. You could even join or create an online community for trading Cricut project ideas and swapping unused materials. Communities can be one of the greatest parts of crafting!

Finally, if you found this book useful in any way, a review on Amazon is always appreciated!

CPSIA information can be obtained
at www.ICGtesting.com
Printed in the USA
LVHW080739241120
672556LV00005B/276

9 781801 156035